# Ocean Frontiers

It's as difficult to survive deep under the oceans as it is in outer space. This book tells the exciting story of how technologists are solving the problems of undersea exploration. Find out about drilling for oil and the job of the deep-sea diver; how submarines and submersibles work, and about the 'aquanauts' who have lived under the sea for days at a time. There are step-by-step instructions on how to make a periscope. And for budding technologists, science comes to life with simple projects and experiments.

**The Viking Press   New York**

## Contents

## Inform

⭐ 

**A star ★ in** 
know-how b
how things w     ook for a star in a box
like the one shown here.

## boxes

**Red boxes** point out projects to make and quick experiments to try. There are simple instructions and diagrams to follow for each one. All you will need are a few easy-to-get materials.

# The oceans are...

**Powerful . . .** giant wave rolls ashore

**Exciting and dangerous . . .** great white shark    **Mysterious . . .** diver at work in the Bahamas

# Rich in energy ... oil-production platform in the North Sea

Though life began beneath the surface of the sea in prehistoric times, human beings now find it very difficult to survive there. It's a hostile environment —as hostile as outer space—yet the seas still have a powerful fascination. Scientists, adventurers and businessmen are exploring beneath the sea to find out its secrets and to extract its wealth. A complex new technology is growing that makes comfort and survival underwater a reality. And that technology is vital. As the food, minerals and energy on land are used up, the place to look for more is—the oceans.

# What's below the surface?

## Our unique planet

When you look at a globe, you can see that the Earth's surface is really seven-tenths water. If a space traveler stopped directly above Tahiti in the South Pacific, he would think our planet was completely covered by water.

The Pacific was once Earth's only ocean. It has been shrinking as other oceans formed, the result of continents moving apart.

Only small groups of islands dot the vast Pacific Ocean.

The other side of the Earth looks much more familiar. Covering most of it are the land masses of Europe, Asia and Africa, with North America just visible at the top.

The Earth is the only planet in our solar system that has oceans. These vast expanses of water, together with oxygen and nitrogen from the air, support all the varied forms of life on our planet.

It isn't hard to understand the attraction of the oceans for the modern explorer. The oceans cover a large part —about seven-tenths—of our planet's surface. And, along with outer space, they are the last great challenge to men who want to explore new areas.

The water that makes up the oceans formed from clouds of steam. These clouds erupted out of the ground as the earth's crust cooled 4500 million years ago. It was a very slow process, and only 180 million years ago did the oceans begin to take shape as we now know them.

Despite the fact that the oceans are such a vital part of our planet, and our lives, we have a very long way to go in unfolding all their secrets.

## The seabed

We do know that the *average* depth of the oceans is about 4000 m (13,123 ft) but this does not mean that the seabed is flat! Hidden from sight is a landscape even more varied than we see on land. There are mountain ranges, vast plains and valleys. One trench goes down to 11,022 m (36,161 ft).

### The continental shelf

From the land, the seabed slopes gently away. The continental shelf is the area of seabed less than 200 m (656 ft) deep surrounding a continent.

### Old volcanoes

Small islands in the middle of the ocean were usually formed by undersea volcanic eruptions. Volcanoes that did not reach the surface are called seamounts.

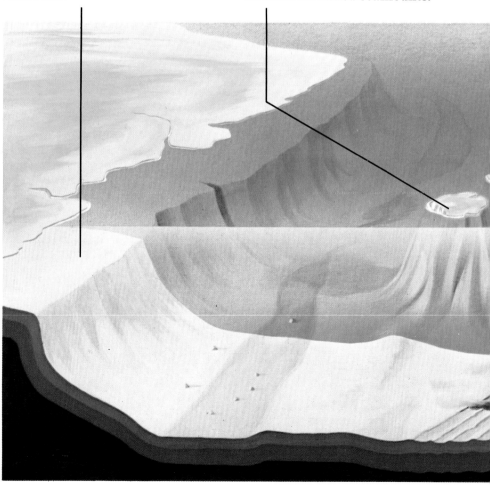

Below: This chart gives you some idea of the progress so far in getting down to the depths of the undersea world. Most exploration takes place in the upper 500 m (1640 ft) of the oceans.

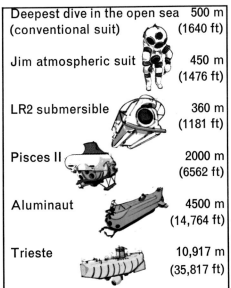

| | |
|---|---|
| Deepest dive in the open sea (conventional suit) | 500 m (1640 ft) |
| Jim atmospheric suit | 450 m (1476 ft) |
| LR2 submersible | 360 m (1181 ft) |
| Pisces II | 2000 m (6562 ft) |
| Aluminaut | 4500 m (14,764 ft) |
| Trieste | 10,917 m (35,817 ft) |

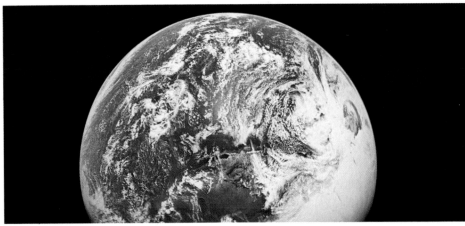

This is what Earth looks like from way out in space. Photographs like this tell scientists a lot about the way oceans and air currents affect our climate. Better weather forecasts can be made.

## Mid-oceanic ridges
There are massive underwater mountain ranges in all the oceans. Some ranges reach a 'height' of 4000 m (13,123 ft) above the seabed, and a width of 4000 km (2480 mi).

## Oceanic trenches
Very little of the total area of the ocean floor lies deeper than 6000 m (19,685 ft). But steep-sided underwater valleys like this can reach depths of 10,000 m (32,808 ft)!

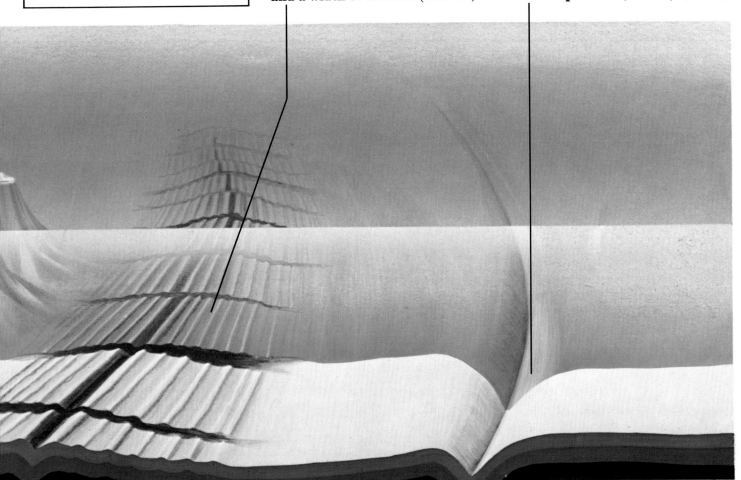

# Early undersea exploration

The first men to venture under the sea had no equipment for breathing underwater. They simply held their breath for as long as possible. Their dives had to be short not longer than a minute or two—and not very deep. To dive underwater they held a large stone, letting it go again when they wanted to come back to the surface. For gathering pearls and sponges, food and even sunken treasure from the sea, this simple system was good enough. During the first century BC, Greek divers salvaging shipwrecks in the eastern Mediterranean were paid according to the depth of water. In 8 m (26 ft) of water, the diver was rewarded with one-half of the goods he had recovered. In 4 m (13 ft) his share was one-third, and in 1 m (3 ft) it was only a tenth.

## The first diving suits

The early diving suits were very simple and most of them would have drowned or suffocated the diver. Nearly all of them showed that the inventors did not understand a very important and basic fact about the underwater world—water exerts pressure on anything under its surface, and the deeper the water, the greater the pressure★.

## ★ Snorkel diving

It's an old idea to breathe underwater through a short tube to the surface. Ancient warriors used to hide from their enemies in rivers, using hollow reeds as breathing tubes.

Have you ever wondered why divers don't simply use longer and longer snorkels to go down deeper? The reason is you can't breathe through a tube much more than 30 cm (12 in) long. If the diver goes down any deeper, the weight of the water will press on his chest and stop him from expanding his lungs properly.

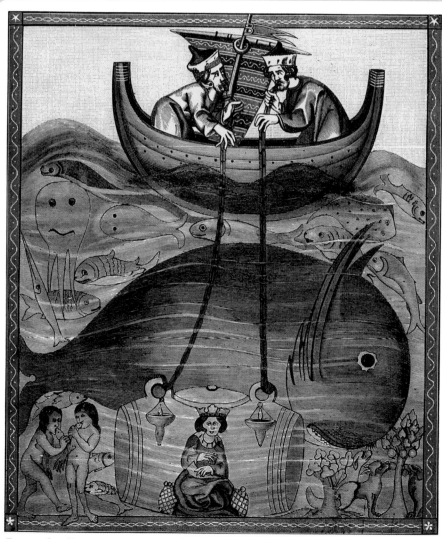

**Legend tells us that Alexander the Great went deep underwater in a glass barrel as long ago as 322 BC. The story goes that he stayed below for three days and nights. How he didn't suffocate we're not told! This is a 13th-century drawing of the scene.**

These designs, printed in a book in 1532, are thought to date back to Roman times. Presumably they were meant to be used by soldiers trying to hide from their enemies underwater. The figure on the left appears to have an air supply from some kind of jug. The one on the right seems to be getting no air!

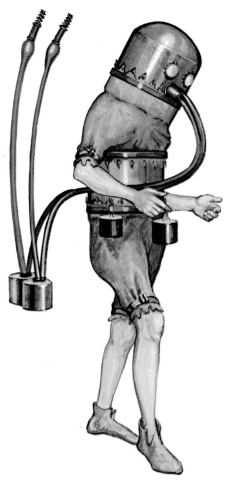

This diving suit was designed by a German named Klingert in 1797. It was made up of an enormous metal helmet and waistband, with a short-sleeved leather jacket and knee-length trousers. The inventor apparently tried the suit out, but without much success. He did not understand that air had to be pumped down to the diver at exactly the same pressure as the water around him.

In 1690, the astronomer Edmund Halley invented the first successful diving bell. If you put an inverted tumbler in water, the water won't rise into it. That's how the bell worked.

# Pioneer divers

Whatever depth he is at, the diver *must* be supplied with air at exactly the same pressure as the water around him. About 150 years ago John Deane and Augustus Siebe devised the first diving suits that did this successfully and safely. Working independently, they produced quite similar designs. John Deane had already invented an airtight helmet and air-pump so that rescuers could go into smoke-filled rooms. With some changes, his smoke helmet was altered into a diving helmet.

## Early experiments

Siebe's first diving helmet was similar. The heavy helmet and breastplate were clamped to a watertight leather jacket that reached down to the waist. Fresh air was pumped down to the diver, and excess air bubbled out from under the jacket. This worked quite well, provided the diver stood upright. If he fell, or bent down too far, his helmet flooded. John Deane himself discovered this in his first tests. It is said that lead boots were introduced at that time to clamp the diver's feet to the ground!

A later model of the suit had a valve on the side of the helmet. It allowed excess air to escape. If the air escaped slowly, the suit tended to blow up so the diver floated up off the bottom. To sink he opened the valve to let out more air. Within a short time Siebe's type of suit and helmet had become almost universal. For over a hundred years it was used as a basis for the improvement of diving methods. In fact, it is still used today by divers working in docks.

### Pumping air down to a diver

**Take a piece of tube about a meter (3 ft) long and a centimeter ($\frac{1}{2}$ in) in diameter. Place one end just under the surface of the water in a bucket. It'll be quite easy to blow bubbles through the tube. Slowly lower the tube into about 50 cm (20 in) of water. Now try to blow down it. It's much more difficult! You've got to blow hard enough to overcome the water pressure at the bottom of the tube. Imagine the pressure in really deep water. What hard work it must have been in the early days pumping air down to divers by hand!**

This diver had, unfortunately, let too much air into his suit.

Left: These two men are working an air pump. The deeper the diver went, the harder they had to pump. Later, power-driven pumps made life easier.

Right: The 'hard-hat' diving suit is still popular with divers working in shallower water on construction projects. Today, a fiberglass helmet is sometimes used instead of the heavy bronze one.

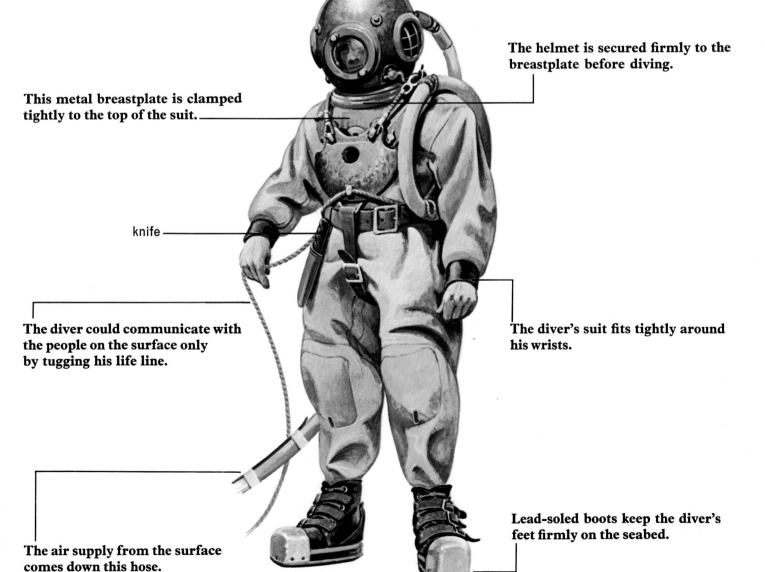

The helmet is secured firmly to the breastplate before diving.

This metal breastplate is clamped tightly to the top of the suit.

knife

The diver could communicate with the people on the surface only by tugging his life line.

The diver's suit fits tightly around his wrists.

The air supply from the surface comes down this hose.

Lead-soled boots keep the diver's feet firmly on the seabed.

9

# Deeper and deeper

In 1977 French divers went as deep as 500 m (1640 ft) during a series of record-breaking experimental dives in the open sea.

To reach these great depths careful research must first be done to see how the human body reacts to high-pressure breathing gases.

## Getting the bends

Some of the possible hazards came to light in quite shallow dives soon after Siebe's suit became popular. When he surfaced after long dives, the diver was often doubled up with pain. This was because of tiny bubbles that appeared in his bloodstream, interfering with his nervous system. Under pressure, extra nitrogen is dissolved in the blood and tissues. This is no problem until the pressure is released, causing *the bends*. It can be avoided by surfacing—or *decompressing*—slowly.

Trying all this out in deep water could be very dangerous, so researchers *simulate* the effects of deep diving in compression chambers on land. The diver doesn't even have to get wet. The pressure inside the chamber can be increased to whatever 'depth' is needed. The effects of the breathing mixture on the diver can be seen by electronic monitoring of his body. Mental and physical tests are used to make sure that the diver will still be able to carry out his work properly, even under great pressure.

This diver is testing a deep-sea diving suit in a tank cooled to 3°C.

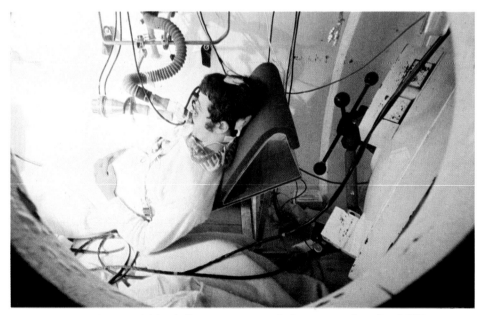

In 1970, experimental 'dry' dives were carried out to a depth of 455 m (1493 ft). This is one of the divers in the compression chamber.

## The bends

Take the top off a carbonated drink bottle very quickly. You will hardly see any bubbles. But if you shake the bottle hard, and take the top off quickly, the drink will froth all over the place. This gives you a good idea of what the bends is all about. The gas is dissolved in the liquid all the time—you just make it leave the liquid much more quickly by shaking the bottle. In the same way, the deep-sea diver will have no problems if he decompresses slowly. If he does get the bends, he must be compressed again quickly.

## Problems of communication

Deep-sea divers breathe a special mixture of oxygen and helium. This is because, under high pressure, a diver breathing air would suffer from 'nitrogen narcosis'. The nitrogen in the air would affect the diver's brain and make him lose control of his actions. To avoid this, the nitrogen is replaced by helium.

However, there are snags. Helium is very expensive. It also takes precious heat away from the diver's body. It affects the speed of sound as well. A diver breathing helium sounds like Donald Duck! There have to be 'speech unscramblers' on the surface so that the crew can understand what the divers say.

## Time for decompression

Charts of decompression times have been drawn up and divers must check them carefully to find out how long they have to decompress after a dive. If a diver spends a long time in a decompression chamber or undersea habitat his body tissues become 'saturated' with inert gas. His blood eventually stops absorbing any more breathing gas. 'Saturation divers' live under pressure for several days rather than decompressing after each dive. See page 14.

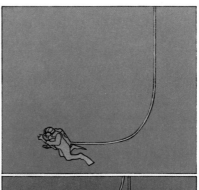

Dives of less than an hour, to approximately 165 feet, can be done by a diver swimming from the surface. He breathes compressed air and decompresses by making frequent stops on his way to the surface. This is a 'bounce dive'.

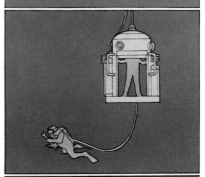

The decompression time for a bounce dive to 165 feet can be as long as three hours! Life can be made more comfortable for the divers by using a small 'wet bell' like this.

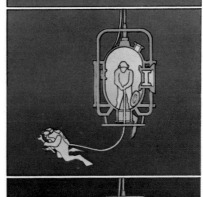

A full-size diving bell is used to reach 120 meters (394 ft). After only an hour at that depth, divers have to decompress for over fifteen hours!

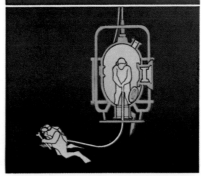

For dives lasting several hours, hundreds of feet down, 'saturation' diving methods are used. Decompression after a 300 meter (976 ft) saturation dive takes nearly a week.

# The modern deep-sea diver

The equipment worn by the deep-sea diver is very different from that of a scuba diver. It isn't self-contained, for a gas cylinder big enough for half an hour, at 10 m (30 ft) down, would run out in less than three minutes at 200 m (655 ft). This is because the gas has to be so highly compressed that the actual quantity used in each breath is much greater. So the gas has to be supplied through a tube called the *umbilical* which reaches back to the bell. In case anything goes wrong with the gas supply, the diver also carries small emergency cylinders—enough to get him back to the bell.

The most recent advances in deep-sea diving are due to the search for oil and gas deep below the North Sea. Conditions 200 m (655 ft) down are difficult, often dangerous, and it is cold, dark and uncomfortable. Not only does a man have to be highly trained for deep diving, but he often has to work as a skilled craftsman or technician. Despite the modern marvels of mechanization and remote control, there are still plenty of jobs in the offshore oil business that need a man on the spot.

Some of the diver's tasks may look simple, like attaching ropes, or cutting or scraping. But they are all made much more difficult just because they have to be done underwater.

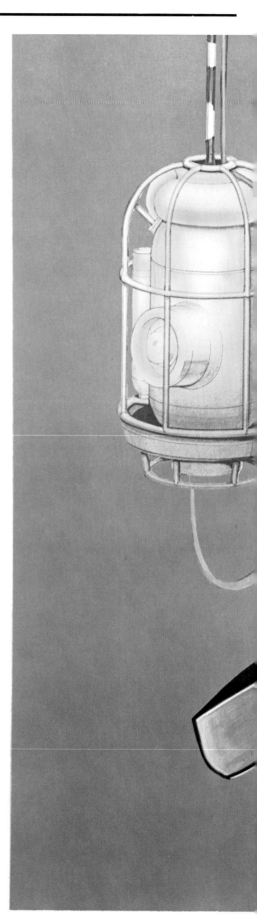

**A diving bell is lowered into the water beside the massive concrete legs of an oil platform. Before the platform could be towed out to sea, divers had to go down to release three anchor chains. Left: This diver is using a power tool to remove scale (rust and marine growths) from welded steel joints. This has to be done before the joints can be inspected for signs of weakness.**

The umbilical carries oxy-helium gas for the diver to breathe, hot water to heat his suit, and his telephone link with the bell and the surface.

Hot water circulates all the time between the diver's suit and his skin to keep him warm. Not only is deep water cold, but the helium in the gas mixture removes heat from his body through his lungs and skin at a much faster rate than if he was exposed to air.

This valve regulates his breathing-gas supply so that it is at the same pressure as the water around him.

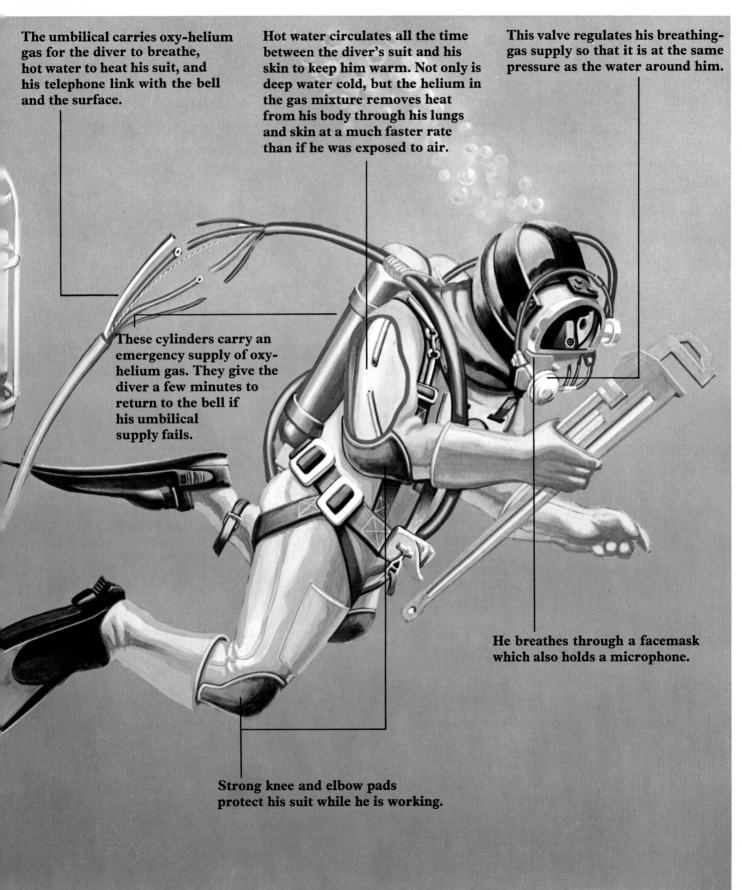

These cylinders carry an emergency supply of oxy-helium gas. They give the diver a few minutes to return to the bell if his umbilical supply fails.

He breathes through a facemask which also holds a microphone.

Strong knee and elbow pads protect his suit while he is working.

# Life under pressure

After long and deep dives, divers have to decompress very slowly to prevent their getting the bends. So, to avoid the need for hours of decompression every time a single dive is made, divers live in pressurized chambers for days or even weeks. At the beginning of a dive, the divers enter the chamber and the hatches are closed tightly behind them. The pressure is then increased to the same pressure that they will experience on the seabed. They travel to and from the seabed in a diving bell, and only decompress much later when the whole job is finished.

## Inside the bell

When they are ready to go underwater, the divers, still under pressure, transfer into the bell. The hatches are sealed and the bell is lowered to the underwater work site. There, the water pressure is equal to the pressure inside, so the bottom hatch can be opened. The divers can then slip into the water and swim out. After a few hours' work the divers return to the surface chamber for food and rest. If the work is urgent, another team can go down to carry on the job.

Life under pressure has its problems. Food and drink have to be passed in through hatches so that pressurization isn't lost. Even simple things like light bulbs have to be protected from the pressure so that they aren't crushed. Outside, teams of technicians work day and night to make sure that all is well for the divers.

**A complex array of chambers like this can support three pairs of divers for day and night work on the seabed. When they are ready to dive, the divers go into the bell through the transfer chamber, along with their assistant, known as the bellman. The bell's hatches are closed and it is lowered to the seabed through a special opening in the deck of the diving barge. The opening is called a 'moon pool'.**

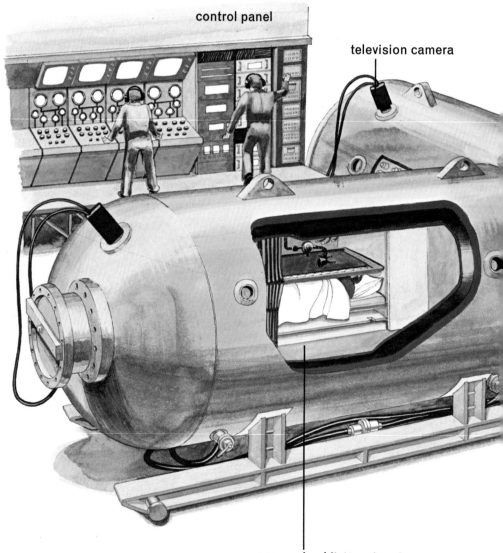

control panel

television camera

pressurized living chamber

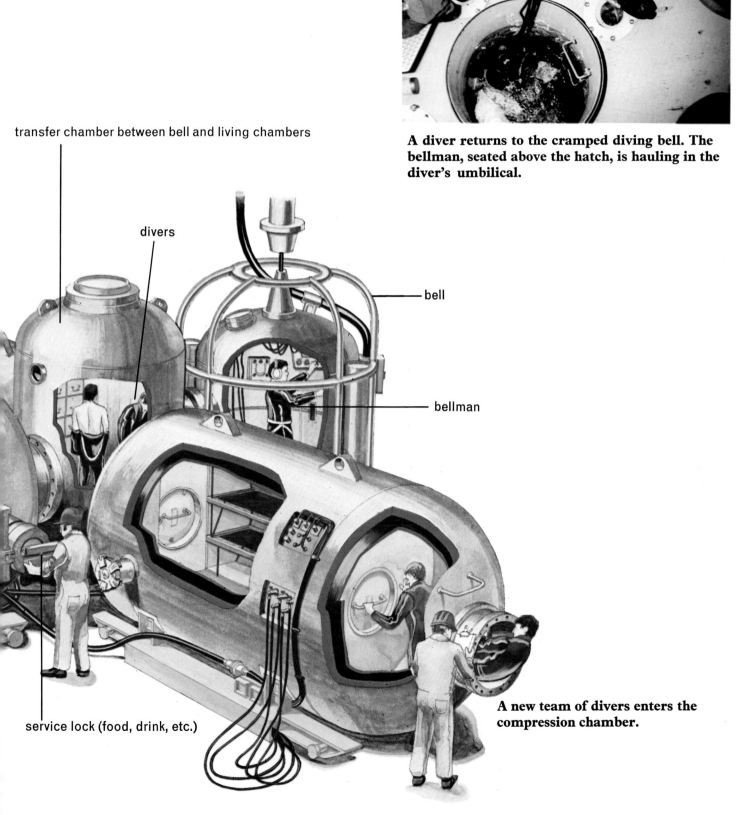

A diver returns to the cramped diving bell. The bellman, seated above the hatch, is hauling in the diver's umbilical.

transfer chamber between bell and living chambers

divers

bell

bellman

service lock (food, drink, etc.)

A new team of divers enters the compression chamber.

# Another approach

Modern deep diving is complex and expensive. But pressurized chambers, bells, helium-based breathing gas, and long hours of decompression are only necessary because of the body's strange reactions to high pressures. So why not make a diving suit that is rigid and protects the diver from the water pressure?

## Normal pressure

This is exactly what the *atmospheric diving suit* does. It is so called because the diver, even hundreds of meters down, breathes air or oxygen at normal pressure. He feels much the same as he would on the surface.

In the 18th and 19th centuries, many would-be inventors tried to make joints, first out of leather and later of corrugated metal bellows. But these were useless in anything but shallow water—the water pressure pressed the bellows together, making them completely impossible to move.

## Ball-and-socket

Just over 50 years ago, while working for a British company, Joseph Peress, a Persian, hit upon the idea of making a *ball-and-socket joint* for an atmospheric suit—almost like our own hip joints★. This led to the best known modern atmospheric suit, Jim, named after Jim Jarratt, the mechanic who made many test dives in the suit for Peress. Jim can work down to nearly 450 m (1476 ft).

## Built-in engine

Deep diving is now vital in the search for oil and gas. Atmospheric diving suits may well become more popular, especially if the search moves into waters too deep for the ordinary diver. Work is going ahead on more advanced suits. Some even have small propellers so that the diver can move about freely! Obviously the atmospheric suit has the disadvantage that the diver can't use his hands directly. But where delicate touch is not needed, doing away with the complicated equipment and medical problems of normal deep diving is a great advantage.

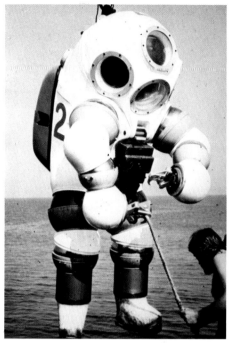

Jim 2 is carefully lowered into the sea. Although the suit weighs half a ton out of the water, the diver can move about quite easily underwater.

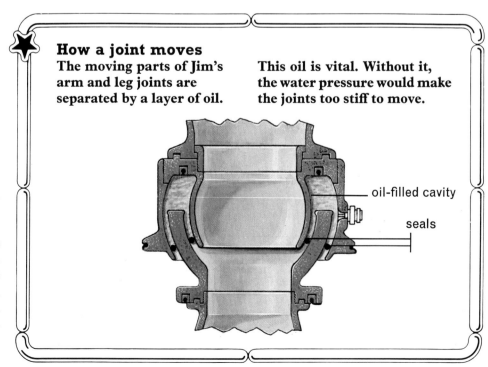

★ **How a joint moves**
The moving parts of Jim's arm and leg joints are separated by a layer of oil.

This oil is vital. Without it, the water pressure would make the joints too stiff to move.

oil-filled cavity

seals

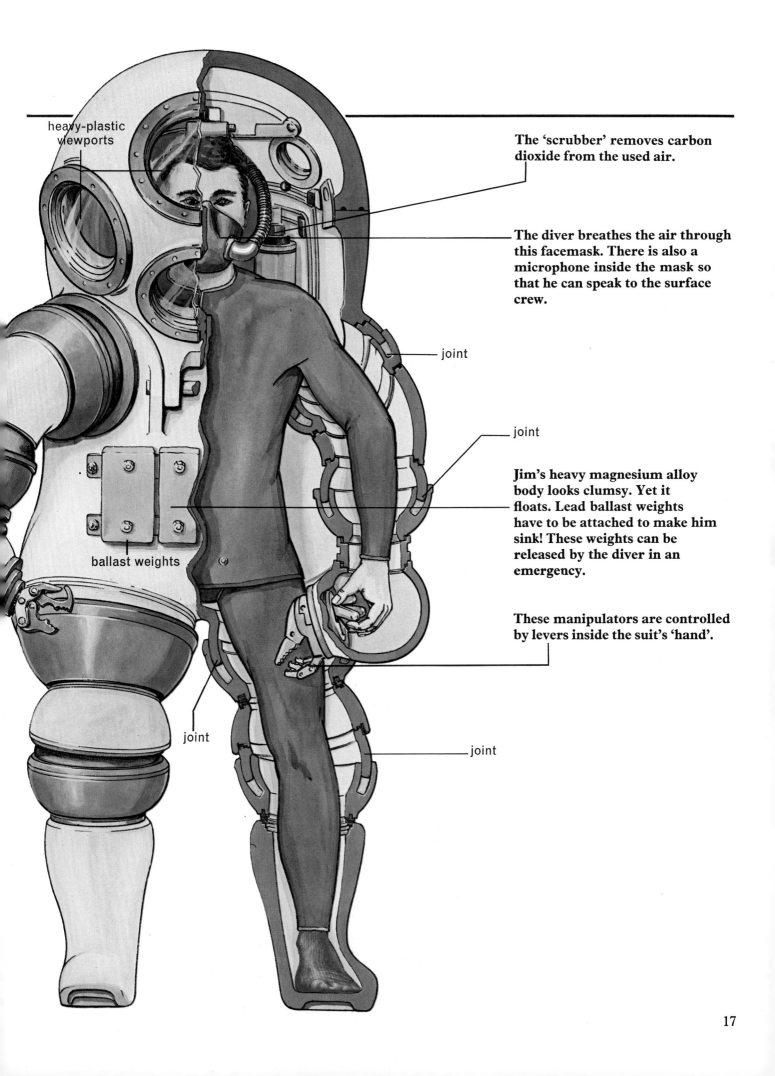

heavy-plastic viewports

The 'scrubber' removes carbon dioxide from the used air.

The diver breathes the air through this facemask. There is also a microphone inside the mask so that he can speak to the surface crew.

joint

joint

ballast weights

Jim's heavy magnesium alloy body looks clumsy. Yet it floats. Lead ballast weights have to be attached to make him sink! These weights can be released by the diver in an emergency.

These manipulators are controlled by levers inside the suit's 'hand'.

joint

joint

# Diving for fun

Captain Jacques Yves Cousteau is best known today for his work on conserving marine life and for his undersea exploration films which appear regularly on TV. But in 1943, with his colleague Emil Gagnan, he made a vital contribution to our freedom to visit the undersea world—he perfected the Aqualung, a trademark name for the widely known *scuba*★ (*s*elf-*c*ontained *u*nderwater *b*reathing *a*pparatus).

## Diving made easier

A diver using a scuba carries his air supply in a lightweight cylinder on his back. Before the Cousteau-Gagnan design, self-contained diving equipment was very difficult to use, and dangerous except in the hands of highly trained experts. While proper training is still vital, the invention of the modern scuba has meant that almost anyone who wants to can explore under the sea.

Scuba divers usually wear *wet suits* made of neoprene foam, even in quite warm water. These suits trap a layer of water between the skin and the material of the suit; the diver's body heat soon warms up this trapped layer. The neoprene provides the insulation that helps keep the diver warm.

A lightweight air cylinder of this size allows the diver to stay under for 40 minutes at 10 m (30 ft). In greater depths, the air doesn't last so long. A double cylinder can be used for longer dives.

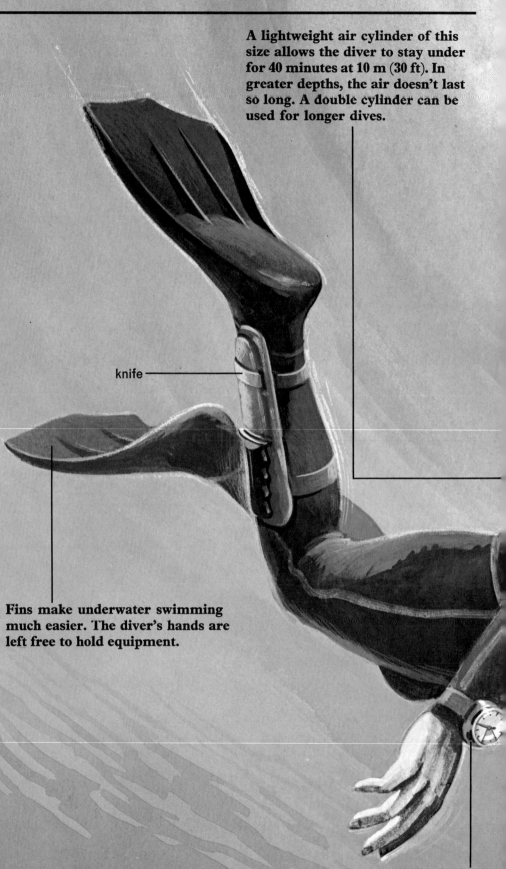

knife

Fins make underwater swimming much easier. The diver's hands are left free to hold equipment.

depth gauge

## How a scuba works

The most important part of a scuba diver's equipment is the demand valve. It controls the air supply from the high-pressure cylinder on his back so that he is supplied with air at *exactly* the same pressure as the water around him. The air is normally shut off by the spring-loaded valve. When the diver breathes in, the diaphragm is sucked in. This moves the lever which opens the valve. When he breathes out, the diaphragm returns to its normal position. The air supply is shut off, and the used air bubbles out into the water.

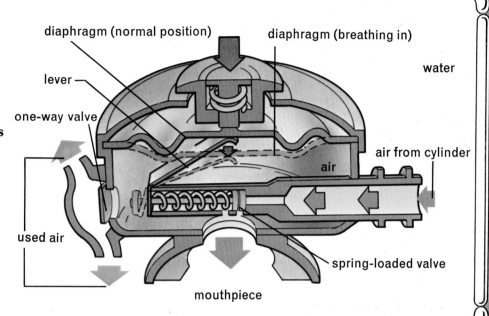

diaphragm (normal position)  diaphragm (breathing in)

lever

water

one-way valve

air from cylinder

air

used air

spring-loaded valve

mouthpiece

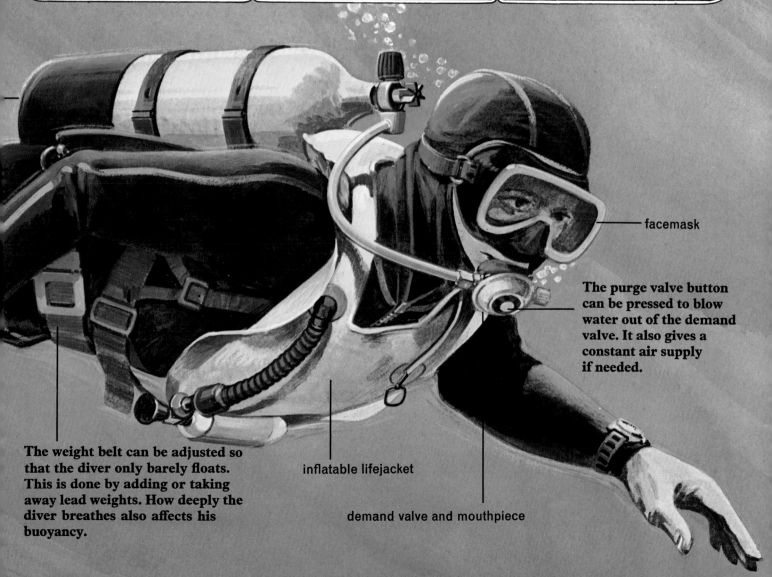

facemask

The purge valve button can be pressed to blow water out of the demand valve. It also gives a constant air supply if needed.

The weight belt can be adjusted so that the diver only barely floats. This is done by adding or taking away lead weights. How deeply the diver breathes also affects his buoyancy.

inflatable lifejacket

demand valve and mouthpiece

# Submerged history

Sunken ships and drowned cities offer valuable clues to historians and archaeologists trying to piece together pictures of the past. Things which have lain underwater for centuries may be better preserved than they would be on land. Since the introduction of the scuba, there has been a tremendous growth of interest in undersea archaeology all around the world.

## Finding the site

Often, shipwrecks can be traced from ancient documents. But they may have broken up, or become covered in mud or sand. If they lie in deep or murky water it can also take time for divers to find them. More and more, underwater archaeologists are turning to inventions like *side-scan sonar* to check what is on the seabed (see pages 34-35).

## Marking the spot

Once the site has been found, it has to be marked so that it can be retraced from the surface every time. A buoy can be attached to the seabed. It is more accurate if the survey ship uses *radio navigation systems* such as Decca or loran (*long-range navigation*). The ship can then position itself directly over the wreck every time it returns there.

**Right: A small diving bell like this can be used as an underwater 'staging post' by divers working on a wreck. It is supplied with air from the surface. When a diver is inside he can save the air in his own scuba. A second diver is carrying the treasures he has found to the bell.**

**Below: A diver comes to the surface carrying an earthenware vessel from an ancient wreck. Archaeologists can learn a lot about the past by studying relics like these.**

## Underwater detective work

1 Metal detectors are very popular with treasure hunters on land. This is an underwater detector. Instead of a bleeper to tell the user that he has found something, this one has a dial which the diver has to watch.

2 This diver is removing debris with an airlift. Air is pumped down from the surface to the nozzle. It rushes back up the tube, sucking water, sand or sediment with it. At the surface, people sieve the material to be sure nothing valuable is missed.

3 A diver can rest in this heavy-plastic diving bell. He can take out his mouthpiece here and breathe air pumped down from the surface.

4 An inflatable bag is an inexpensive and easy way of lifting things to the surface. The diver swims down with the bag empty, fixes it to whatever he wants to lift, and pumps it up with air.

5 Sketching is a very useful way of keeping a record of what the diver sees. He draws with a waterproof crayon on a piece of white plastic.

6 A frame of poles is used to divide the site up into small square sections. Each square is numbered to make it easy for the divers to remember from where each relic was lifted.

7 A photograph of each square taken through a frame like this gives a good record of the finds.

# Undersea raiders

Submarines were first developed as war machines, rather than as a means of finding out more about the undersea world. Being able to attack ships secretly, and from below, gives an obvious advantage over the enemy. Some of the early submarines were powered only by gasoline and diesel engines. The trouble was that they needed a constant supply of fresh air for the engines to operate. These submarines could only dive as deep as a snorkel tube to the surface would let them!

## Small but effective

The modern diesel-electric submarine doesn't have this problem. The electric motors are driven by rechargeable batteries, just like car batteries. The submarine has to come up for air only to run the diesel engines which drive generators for charging up the batteries. The 'conventional' submarine isn't as powerful as its rival, the nuclear giant. But in certain cases its small size is an advantage. Because it can operate in a smaller area, it still has a vital part to play in the world's navies.

### First 'torpedo sub'

This wooden, egg-shaped one-man submarine was built by an American in 1776. The pilot worked its two propellers and the rudders by means of handles inside. It carried an explosive charge in a watertight box on the outside. A drill bore into the wooden hull of a ship and attached the explosive.

snorkel for fresh air

portholes

explosive charge

rudder

drill

propellers

buoyancy controls

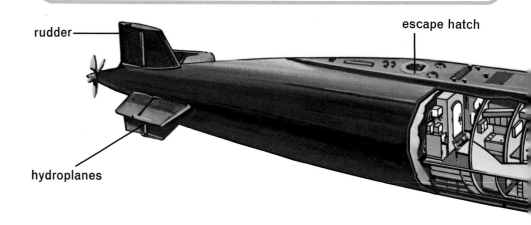

rudder

escape hatch

hydroplanes

## Steam submarines

This extraordinary steam-driven submarine was built by an English clergyman, the Rev. George W. Garrett, in 1879. It could travel underwater for 16 km (10 m) at about 4 km/h (2 knots). Since the boilers couldn't be used when the submarine was submerged, a clever method of storing heat was used. Steam produced by boilers on the surface was stored over large hot-water tanks for the underwater journey. Unfortunately, the submarine was not around for long. It sank before its trials were complete.

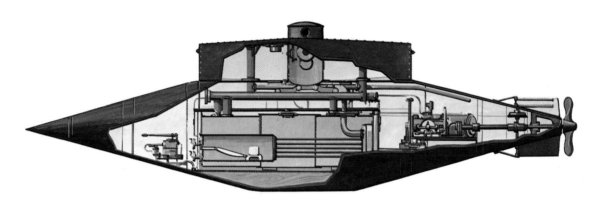

## Giant batteries

A diesel-electric submarine is generally much smaller than its nuclear-powered cousin and it isn't as fast. It has to surface to run its diesel engines and to charge the batteries, so it cannot stay submerged for so long. But it is much cheaper to build and operate. Naturally, the crew's quarters are much more cramped than on a nuclear submarine. This drawing shows the 1200-ton French submarine *Agosta,* built in 1975. It is powered by two diesel engines and a bank of huge batteries.

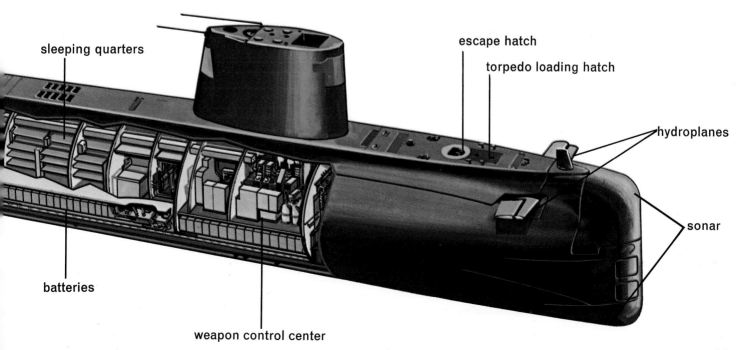

sleeping quarters

escape hatch

torpedo loading hatch

hydroplanes

sonar

batteries

weapon control center

# The nuclear submarine

Nuclear power is simply the power produced by harnessing the tremendous energy of an atomic explosion. The explosion doesn't actually happen, of course—the *nuclear reactor* is designed so that the power is produced smoothly and controllably. Just half a kilogram (about a pound) of uranium can produce as much energy as thousands of tons of coal!

The great advantage of nuclear power is that the submarine doesn't need to come to the surface to charge its batteries. The unlimited supply of power also means that more equipment and machinery can be driven. Electricity is used to produce oxygen and fresh water from sea water. Heating, lighting, and nearly all the comforts of a surface ship can be taken for granted.

Nuclear submarines also have the advantage of speed. They can travel underwater as fast as 45 km/h (25 knots)—so fast in fact that they have to bank when turning, almost like an aircraft. The hydroplanes and rudder control all the submarine's movements★. In fact the pilot's position looks a lot like an airliner's cockpit but without windows. Nuclear submarines can carry torpedoes or long-range nuclear missiles. Submerged around-the-world missions or trips under polar icecaps are well within their capabilities. The only reason for coming to the surface at all is to stock up on food or to change the crew.

## Make a periscope

**You will need:**
**2 handbag mirrors 9 cm × 6.5 cm**
**(3½ in × 2½ in)**
**Large sheet of cardboard**
**Pencil and ruler**
**Scissors**
**Glue**

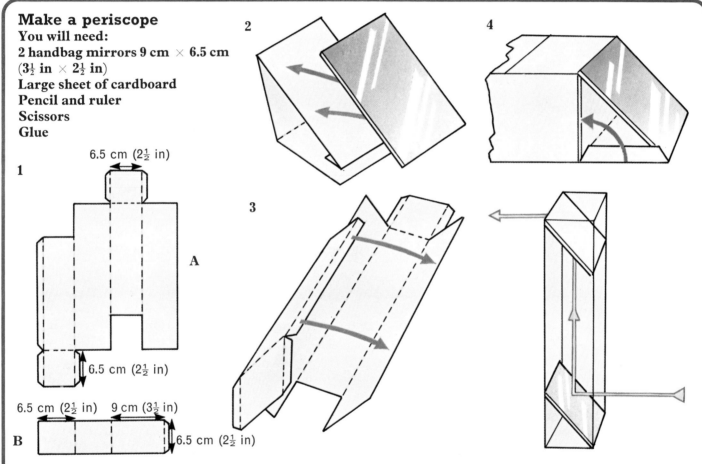

1. **Draw the shapes shown above on the cardboard. Draw shape A once and shape B twice.**
2. **Cut out shape B. Fold the card inward along the dotted lines. Glue the tab and press it on the other edge to make a triangle. Glue mirror to the long side of the triangle. Repeat with the second shape B.**
3. **Cut out shape A. Fold the** card inward along the dotted lines. Glue the tab on the long side and press the edges together to make a square tube (a cardboard flap will project at each end).
4. Glue the triangles you've made from shape B onto the cardboard flaps, with the mirrors facing away from the tube. Fold the cardboard flaps inward along the dotted lines so that the mirrors lie inside the tube. Glue the side tabs of the flaps to the inside ends of the tube. Now stand behind a fence and poke the end of the periscope up over the top. Look in the mirror at the bottom and you will be able to see what is happening on the other side.

Nuclear submarines are able to pass right underneath the polar ice cap. An echo sounder is used to pick a safe path beneath the ice. This is the British submarine *HMS Sovereign* at the North Pole. The ice was thin enough for it to break surface.

In the operations room members of the crew keep a constant watch on the complex control panels. Here, they plot the exact whereabouts of other vessels, and control the missiles.

A modern submarine carries a huge array of electronic equipment to 'look' around above and below the water. Despite this, the periscope is still a vital piece of equipment.

## Diving and surfacing

When a submarine is on the surface, its ballast tanks are empty (1). To dive, these tanks are filled with water (2 and 3). To come up again, high-pressure air is blown into the tanks to start emptying them (4). At the surface, fresh air is pumped into the tanks to empty them (5 and 6).

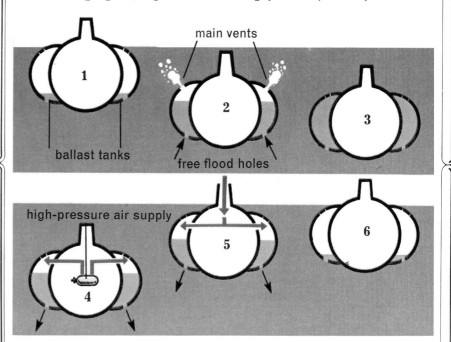

main vents

ballast tanks

free flood holes

high-pressure air supply

## Flying through water

Besides the main ballast tanks, a submarine has trim tanks. By adjusting the latter, the vessel keeps a level course when it is fully submerged. The captain can move the hydroplanes up and down to climb or dive. They work just like the elevators on an aircraft.

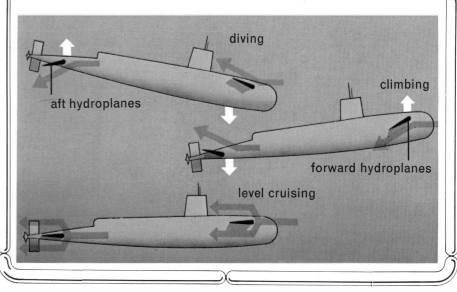

diving

climbing

aft hydroplanes

forward hydroplanes

level cruising

# The bathysphere and bathyscaphe

The bathysphere was a vessel for really deep diving. It was built by two Americans, William Beebe, a marine zoologist, and Otis Barton, an engineer. Beebe wanted to study creatures living deep in the oceans, but at that time he could only have dived to about 25 m (80 ft) without the bathysphere.

The bathysphere had to be lowered on a steel cable from a barge on the surface.

It had a telephone line for Beebe and Barton to keep in touch with their support crew. A heavy electric power cable supplied their searchlight, which was actually inside the bathysphere. From 1930 to 1934, they carried out a series of famous dives in the Caribbean Sea, including a record-breaking one to 923 m (3028 ft). They were the first human beings to see that the under-water world below 300 m (1000 ft) was permanently dark.

## The bathyscaphe

A few years later the Swiss physicist and high-altitude balloonist Auguste Piccard devised the bathyscaphe. The name literally means 'deep boat'. It was simply a crew sphere, just like the bathysphere, hanging from a massive

### Why a sphere ?

**A sphere only 1½ m (5 ft) in diameter hardly seems the best cabin shape for two men to live in for several hours at a time under the sea. But tests show that the rounded shape of a bathysphere is the best possible design for standing up to outside pressure. The bathysphere was made of steel 4 cm (1½ in) thick and weighed 2½ tons. When completely submerged, the pull on the steel cable supporting it was still nearly a ton! Without a strong cable and a powerful winch on their barge at the surface, the undersea explorers would have been in grave danger.**

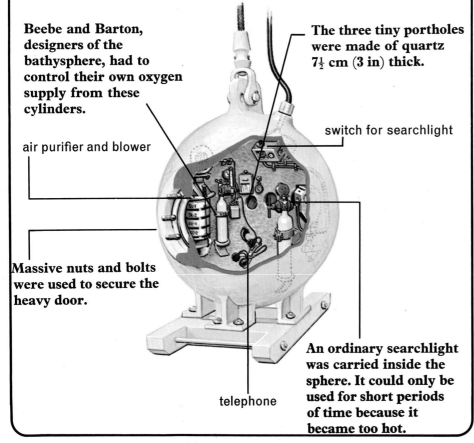

**Beebe and Barton, designers of the bathysphere, had to control their own oxygen supply from these cylinders.**

air purifier and blower

**The three tiny portholes were made of quartz 7½ cm (3 in) thick.**

switch for searchlight

**Massive nuts and bolts were used to secure the heavy door.**

telephone

**An ordinary searchlight was carried inside the sphere. It could only be used for short periods of time because it became too hot.**

**This float is filled with about 182,000 liters (40,000 gallons) of gasoline at the surface. Gasoline is let out, and replaced by water, to make the bathyscaphe sink.**

**This probe is lowered to find out if the seabed is solid.**

float, but it could go even deeper and did not need to be tied to a barge. In a way it was similar to the balloon that Piccard knew so well. The balloon and the bathyscaphe both make use of Archimedes' principle, which is that a container of light fluid immersed in a heavier fluid will tend to float. In the same way as the hydrogen or helium-filled balloon supports a gondola and its crew, the gasoline-filled float of the bathyscaphe displaces enough heavier sea water to support the sphere.

These men were the pioneers of underwater vessels for peacetime use. Even today there are only two bathyscaphes in the world capable of diving deeper than 6000 m (20,000 ft). On the other hand, there is usually no great need to dive deeper than this.

**In January 1960 the bathyscaphe *Trieste* dived into the deepest ocean trench in the world—the 10,917 m (35,817 ft) Challenger Deep in the Pacific. It was crewed by Jacques Piccard (son of Auguste) and Lieutenant Don Walsh of the U.S. Navy.**

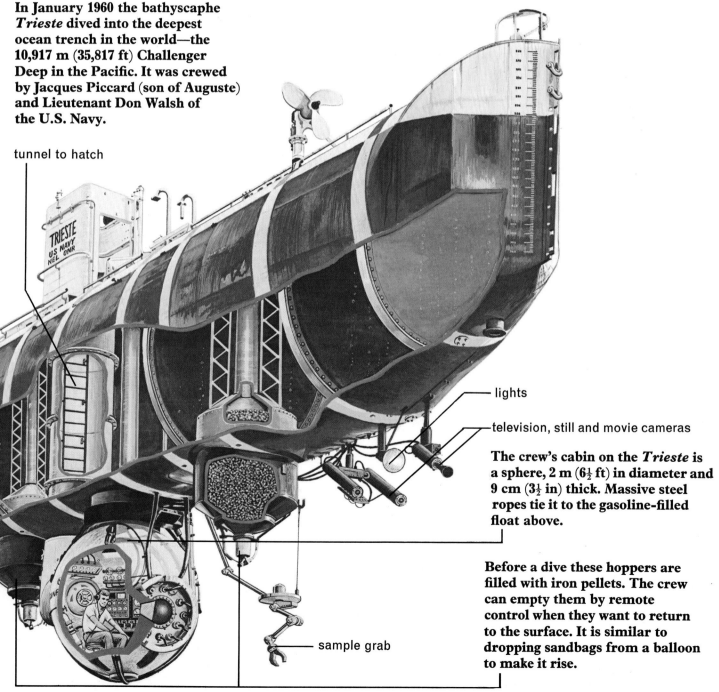

tunnel to hatch

lights

television, still and movie cameras

**The crew's cabin on the *Trieste* is a sphere, 2 m (6½ ft) in diameter and 9 cm (3½ in) thick. Massive steel ropes tie it to the gasoline-filled float above.**

**Before a dive these hoppers are filled with iron pellets. The crew can empty them by remote control when they want to return to the surface. It is similar to dropping sandbags from a balloon to make it rise.**

sample grab

# The modern submersible

The word 'submersible' really means any underwater craft, but it is now usually used for the miniature submarines which are designed as underwater workboats. These carry one or more men as crew and a vast range of tools and instruments.

These submersibles are rarely longer than 10 m (30 ft). They are electrically driven, all the power coming from large banks of batteries carried in watertight pods. These batteries are usually sufficient for missions lasting half a day, but the crew's own life-support system can last for several days in an emergency.

The pilot uses the thrusters, hydro-planes, rudder and the buoyancy system to control his craft. Besides the main thruster at the tail, he can use side and bow thrusters to move around in small spaces.

## Seabed ferry

A recent design is the *diver lock-out*

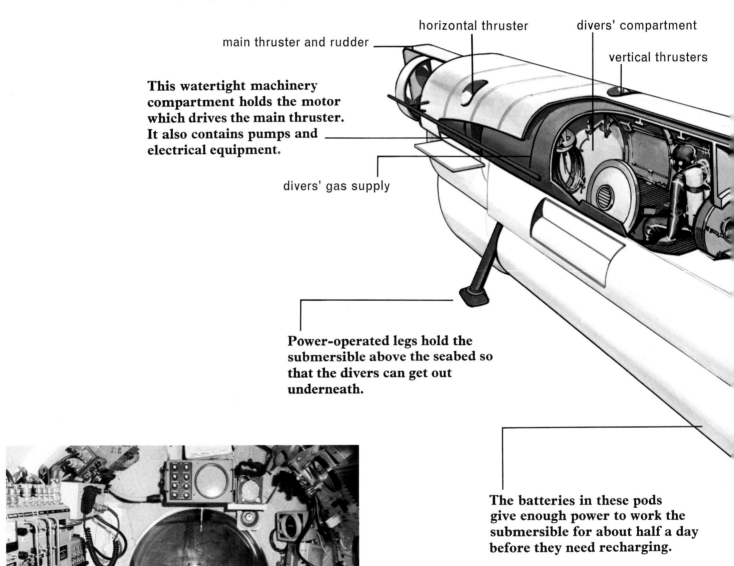

horizontal thruster

divers' compartment

main thruster and rudder

vertical thrusters

**This watertight machinery compartment holds the motor which drives the main thruster. It also contains pumps and electrical equipment.**

divers' gas supply

**Power-operated legs hold the submersible above the seabed so that the divers can get out underneath.**

**The batteries in these pods give enough power to work the submersible for about half a day before they need recharging.**

**The submersible pilot and his observer sit in this cramped space. The big plastic viewport in the center of the picture gives a clear view ahead.**

submersible. A pressurized compartment behind the normal, unpressurized, crew's compartment is used to ferry divers from the surface to the seabed just like a diving bell. This can be more convenient for the divers because a supervisor in the front of the submersible can see what they are doing.

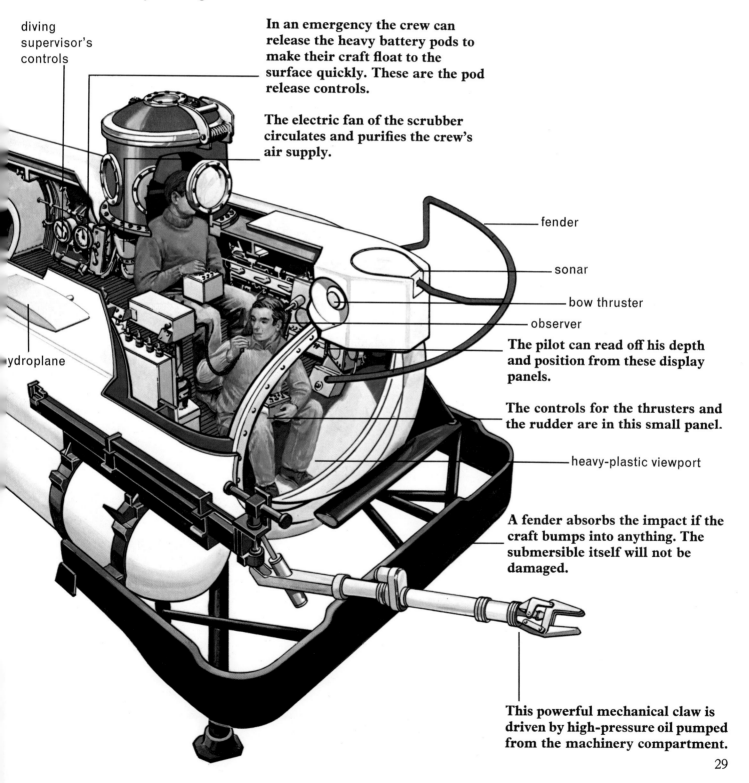

diving supervisor's controls

**In an emergency the crew can release the heavy battery pods to make their craft float to the surface quickly. These are the pod release controls.**

**The electric fan of the scrubber circulates and purifies the crew's air supply.**

fender

sonar

bow thruster

observer

**The pilot can read off his depth and position from these display panels.**

**The controls for the thrusters and the rudder are in this small panel.**

heavy-plastic viewport

ydroplane

**A fender absorbs the impact if the craft bumps into anything. The submersible itself will not be damaged.**

**This powerful mechanical claw is driven by high-pressure oil pumped from the machinery compartment.**

# Submersibles at work

Submersibles rely on limited battery power, so they have to operate from a mother ship. The mother ship has handling equipment and storage space for the submersible itself. It also has maintenance workshops, facilities for recharging batteries and electronic gadgets for keeping track of the submersible when it is underwater.

Companies that use submersibles have perfected methods so that they can launch and retrieve their craft even in really bad weather. A submersible is often handled with the mother ship steaming ahead slowly to keep the tethering cable taut all the time. The *gantry* which lowers and raises the submersible is operated by huge *hydraulic rams*. The gantry automatically adjusts to the pitching movement of the ship in rough seas.

Submersibles operating in the North Sea don't have to dive much deeper than about 500 m (1640 ft). Some submersibles can go deeper, but they need to be stronger to withstand the greater pressure. They are also more complicated, expensive and heavy.

## Sub-sea work platform

Within their depth limits, submersibles can carry out a huge variety of tasks. Sometimes they dive just to carry out surveys with underwater television cameras, backed up by the crew's commentaries. They can be mobile underwater work platforms, capable of lifting and moving heavy objects★, drilling and cutting, and even burying cables in trenches dug with powerful water jets.

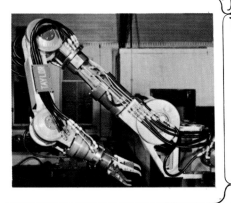

★ **Remote controlled arm**
Complex mechanical claws, known as manipulators, can lift things outside the submersible. A claw has so many joints in it that it can move about almost like a human arm. The manipulator is operated hydraulically.

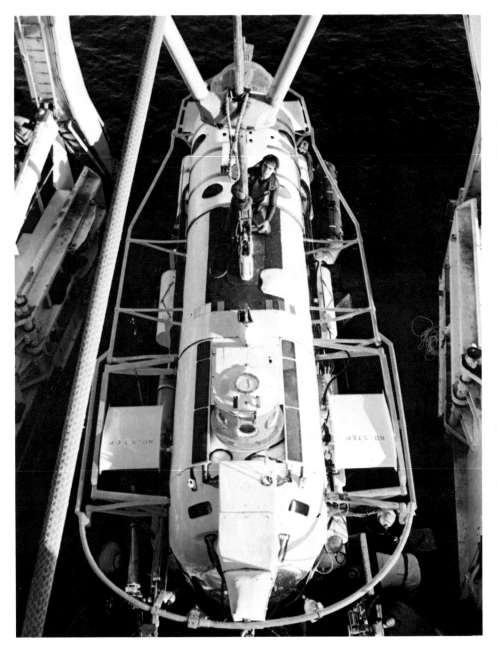

On the right you can see a diver lock-out submersible being lifted from the water.

The Pisces class of submersibles has been used successfully all over the world. Pisces I was the first submersible to start work in the North Sea in 1969.

The divers in the picture below are preparing to get Pisces III out of the sea in rough weather. Submersible operators have practiced ways of handling their craft safely even in difficult conditions like these.

# Undersea robots

*Unmanned submersibles* can be used when the job is simple or when conditions are too dangerous for divers or manned submersibles to go down. They carry tools and instruments just like a manned submersible. The operator in the mother ship guides the craft by remote control, using underwater television and electronic navigation equipment.

## Remote control

You have probably heard about remote controlled aircraft and space probes. These use radio to keep in contact with Earth. Radio waves don't travel in water, so a long cable, the umbilical, links the unmanned craft to the surface. This carries electric power for the thrusters and commands for speed, direction and depth. All the tools, such as drills or grabs, are controlled through the umbilical. TV pictures and navigational information go the other way up to the operator's control panel.

## Built-in buoyancy

Unmanned submersibles carry floats—hollow tanks, or blocks of rigid foam—so that the craft *just* floats on the surface. From then on, the thrusters are used to control every movement.

In an emergency, the operator has a control that cuts the umbilical near the craft. The built-in buoyancy of the floats allows the submersible to rise to the surface where it can be picked up by the mother ship.

**In the control room**
If you were sitting in front of the operator's controls for an unmanned submersible, this is what you'd see. The television screens show you the view in front of the submersible. All the other dials tell you exactly what is happening to the complex machinery on the craft. The joy sticks on the control panel operate the thrusters and manipulators, and also steer the mounts the cameras sit on.

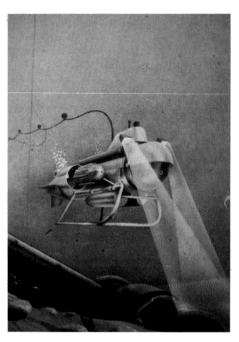

**ANGUS is a submersible cleverly made out of an old torpedo. Instead of carrying its equipment in watertight boxes on an open frame, everything is contained in the tubular body. At the front end is a curved heavy-plastic viewport where the cameras are placed.**

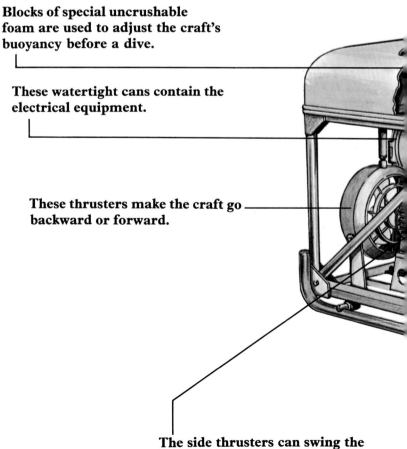

**The umbilical cable connects the unmanned submersible to the control position on the surface.**

**Blocks of special uncrushable foam are used to adjust the craft's buoyancy before a dive.**

**These watertight cans contain the electrical equipment.**

**These thrusters make the craft go backward or forward.**

**The side thrusters can swing the craft around.**

The CETUS unmanned submersible is edged over the stern of a survey ship, ready to begin a new task.

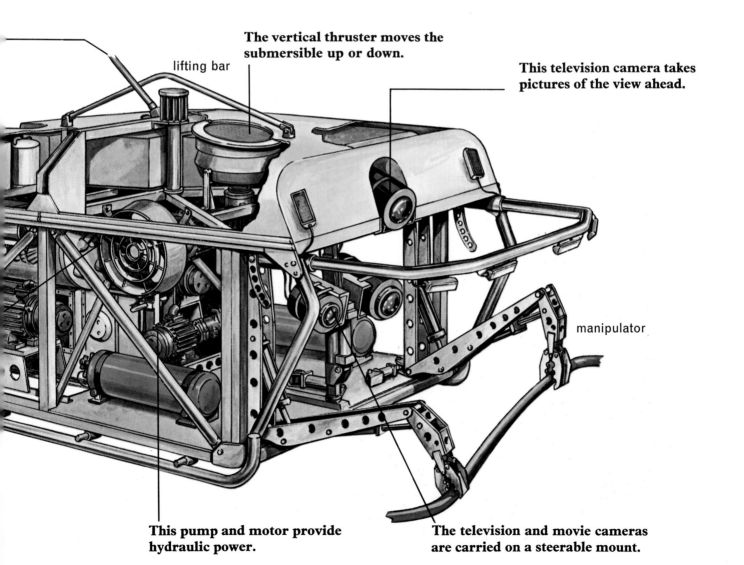

The vertical thruster moves the submersible up or down.

lifting bar

This television camera takes pictures of the view ahead.

manipulator

This pump and motor provide hydraulic power.

The television and movie cameras are carried on a steerable mount.

# Underwater sound

Scientists can survey the planets using telescopes and space probes. But it's very difficult to form a picture of the seabed. Most of it is hidden from view. Fortunately, sound travels very well in water. When sound is beamed down at the seabed, an echo bounces back. This simple fact is used to map the seabed and also to help underwater craft find their way around.

## Mapping the ocean floor

Side-scan sonar (standing for *s*onic *n*avigation and *r*anging device) beams down a fan-shaped strip of sound from a *deep-tow vehicle*. The echoes received are picked up by a machine to be turned into a map of the seabed. Small tows are used in shallow waters but some are big enough to take in hundreds of square kilometers of deep-ocean floor in a single sweep.

## Finding the way

When a submersible pilot goes deeper than 300 m (1000 ft), he has to steer in total darkness. But by using an *acoustic underwater navigation system*, he can place the submersible within a meter of where he wants to be.

Before a submersible dives, the mother ship drops *transponders* to the bottom. A transponder is a small underwater beacon that makes a high-pitched pinging noise. The submersible detects the various pings and a small computer can then find out exactly where the submersible is in relation to the transponders.

A small side-scan sonar vehicle is lowered from a survey ship.

**Seabed survey**

**Side-scan sonar is used to survey the seabed for several purposes. Oil companies might need to know what is down there before laying a pipeline. Archaeologists can use sonar to trace underwater remains. Geologists tracing the history of the Earth need to study the ocean floors. The picture below shows how the deep-tow vehicle is drawn behind the ship over the survey site. The sonar equipment is carried in this way to avoid interference from the ship's engines and propellers. The sonar only provides a picture of the seabed— it doesn't tell us how deep anything is. An echo sounder on the survey ship checks the depth.**

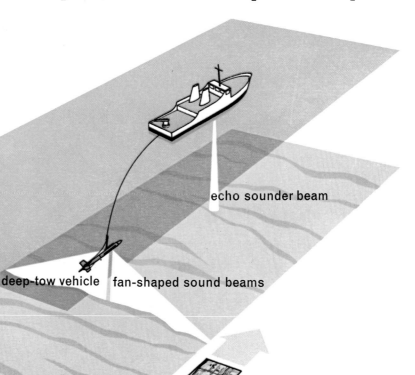

echo sounder beam

deep-tow vehicle    fan-shaped sound beams

**A machine on the survey ship prints out a chart like this. It shows the peaks and troughs on the sea-bed.**

## Voices under the sea

The first telegraph cable across the Atlantic was finished in 1866. Before it could be laid, surveys were taken of the seabed along the route the cable would follow. Today, the oceans are crossed by many cables carrying telephone and telex messages to all parts of the world. Ships like the *Cable Venture* go to sea with hundreds of miles of cable coiled up in the hold, ready to be laid.

## Underwater navigation

A submersible pilot might have to steer his submersible to one particular spot on the seabed, or keep an exact check on his position during a pipeline survey. A specially developed acoustic navigation system, like the one below, allows the pilot to measure his position accurately. Transponders are dropped to the seabed from the mother ship before the submersible dives. At the end of the mission a special coded signal will be picked up by the transponders. This releases them and they float to the surface to be picked up.

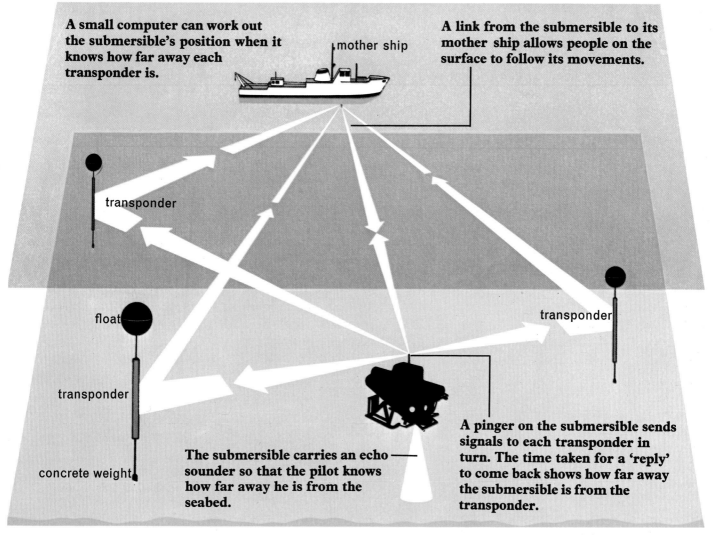

A small computer can work out the submersible's position when it knows how far away each transponder is.

mother ship

A link from the submersible to its mother ship allows people on the surface to follow its movements.

transponder

float

transponder

concrete weight

transponder

The submersible carries an echo sounder so that the pilot knows how far away he is from the seabed.

A pinger on the submersible sends signals to each transponder in turn. The time taken for a 'reply' to come back shows how far away the submersible is from the transponder.

# Seeing underwater

If you open your eyes while swimming underwater, everything looks blurred. This is simply because your eyes are meant to work when they are in contact with air, not water. Fortunately there is a simple answer to this problem. Divers wear facemasks so that there is an airspace in front of their eyes★. The same problem applies to cameras adapted for underwater use. Very few are specially designed to work with their lenses in the water. Usually, an ordinary 'dry-land' camera is mounted in a watertight housing, with a flat, transparent window at the front. Everything the camera 'sees' is magnified, so it is focused differently.

## In the dark

Light doesn't travel very well through water either. If you can see 30 m (100 ft) underwater, for example, in clear Mediterranean waters, then visibility is very good. On land, that's how far you could see in a fog. The deeper the water, the darker it gets. Even in the clearest water, in broad daylight, it is completely dark below 300 m (1000 ft). Artificial lights have to be used to see down, but then it can be like

This diver is examining a ship's propeller with the aid of a modern lightweight television camera and light. The camera is attached to the sides of his helmet. Low-light television cameras can even be used without any lights at all. Most submersibles carry underwater television cameras too.

## ★ What a diver sees

For a diver to see an object underwater, rays of light have to travel from the water, through glass and into the airspace in front of the diver's eyes. At each boundary the light is deflected (bent). This makes everything look nearer and bigger than it actually is, but at least there is no blur, and the diver sees clearly!

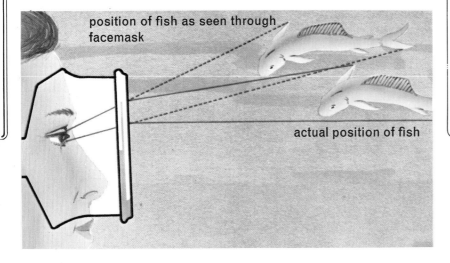

position of fish as seen through facemask

actual position of fish

## Seeing in the dark

Using a powerful light underwater doesn't always help you see very far. Most of the light is reflected from particles of debris in the water. Not enough of the light reaches what you want to see.

The 'flying eyeball' is a small, unmanned, underwater craft fitted with a television camera and lights. Four small propellers allow the operator on the surface to move it around in tight spaces. A cable linking the craft to equipment on the surface carries command signals and television pictures. One 'eyeball' has worked nearly 6000 m (20,000 ft) down!

trying to use car headlights in a fog★.
The underwater television cameras
used by divers are very compact. Some
can even be mounted on a diver's
helmet. Other types are made to stand
up to the pressure of very deep ocean
use and can be operated from the surface. *Low light* television cameras can
even give a picture when it looks
completely dark to the human eye.

**Many modern underwater photographs are as clear as ones taken on land. This diver is taking pictures of corals with a watertight camera housing and flash. An ordinary camera is mounted behind the special lens of the housing. The camera has to be focused differently underwater, otherwise things look magnified.**

# Rescue and safety

The exciting underwater world can be hazardous. The diving crew are carefully trained to prevent accidents.

## Doctors under pressure

Although decompression times have been carefully worked out, there is always a chance of a diver suffering from the bends. If that happens, he must be put back in a compression chamber as soon as possible to be recompressed under close medical care. For a deep-sea diver, working 'in saturation' the problems can be even worse. A diver who falls ill, or is injured while diving, must be brought to the surface immediately in the bell and receive medical attention *while still under pressure*. This is simply because it takes so long—up to several days—to decompress after a deep dive.

## The DSRV

Most submersibles have sufficient life support equipment to keep the crew alive for several days. This gives time to send down divers, or other submersibles, should they get into difficulties. In the case of a huge vessel, like a nuclear submarine, lifting it to the surface isn't always possible. Because of this the U.S. Navy is building a series of DSRVs (Deep Submergence Rescue Vehicles) which can work down to 1500 m (4921 ft). The DSRV will fit in the hold of a freighter aircraft and can operate from a surface vessel or from a nuclear submarine.

**Right: CURV is an unmanned rescue submersible which has made quite a name for itself. The letters stand for Cable-controlled Underwater Recovery Vehicle. In 1966, CURV lifted an H-bomb from a crashed bomber. Then in 1973, it played a vital part in rescuing the stricken Pisces III submersible. The Pisces was stranded helplessly on the seabed 500 m (1640 ft) down. The crew managed to survive 3½ days in their cramped cabin while rescue attempts were made. CURV made the final, successful bid and attached a lifting line to the Pisces.**

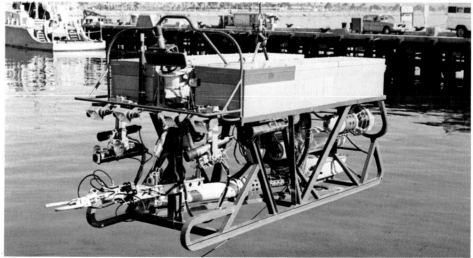

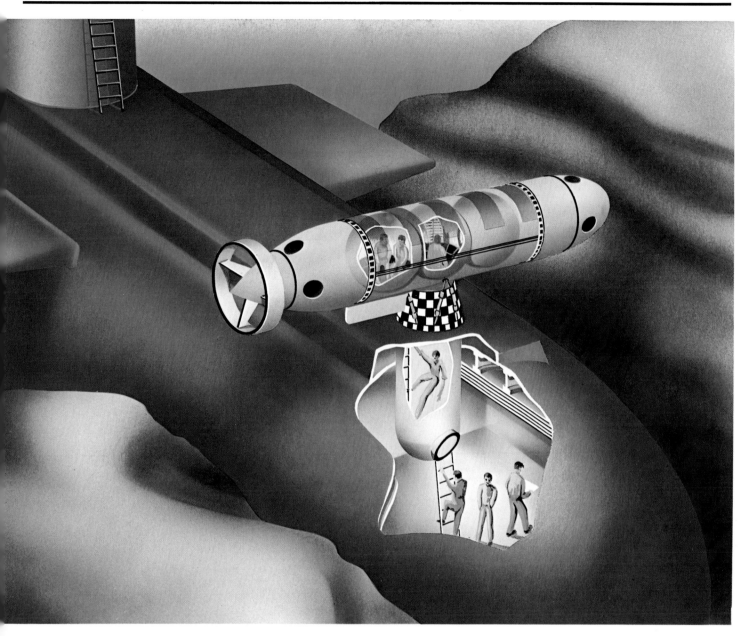

## World-wide rescue service

The DSRV is a submersible especially designed to rescue crews from other underwater craft, especially nuclear submarines. It is 15 m (49 ft) long, 2½ m (8 ft) in diameter, and it weighs 30 tons. An aircraft like the C-141 Starlifter can transport it anywhere in the world within 24 hours of a disaster. Beneath the cigar-shaped outer covering of the DSRV are three compartments. The front one is for the pilot and co-pilot. The other two can carry as many as 24 sub-mariners at a time to safety.

A dive normally lasts six hours. But if the DSRV itself gets stranded, its life-support system can keep the people inside alive for 16 days—more than long enough for help to arrive. The DSRV can operate from the surface, or it can use another nuclear submarine as an underwater staging post. The bell-shaped skirt beneath the middle of a DSRV's hull connects directly to the main hatch on the center sphere. It fits exactly on the standard-sized escape hatch used on nuclear submarines.

# Modern ocean research

Oceanography is the modern science that finds out about all aspects of the sea—tides, currents and temperatures, the creatures living in it, and even the seabed itself. Experts in all branches of science work together to help solve some of the ocean's mysteries.

## Floating laboratory

A modern research ship is really a floating laboratory. Besides a standard crew it carries scientists and their instruments anywhere in the world. Many of the sampling and measuring instruments used by the scientists give continuous readings which can be recorded on paper charts or magnetic tape. The computer is a vital part of the ship's equipment. It brings together all the information being gathered during the voyage and relates it to the ship's position and the weather conditions.

The 2700-ton research ship *Discovery* carries 45 crew and 21 scientists. It is equipped to carry out ocean research almost anywhere in the world. On board are some of the most up-to-date instruments used in oceanography.

## The Data Buoy

Unmanned buoys out at sea can take measurements automatically. The Data Buoy can collect information about what's going on under the sea and on the surface. It even keeps data about the weather. The results are radioed back to shore.

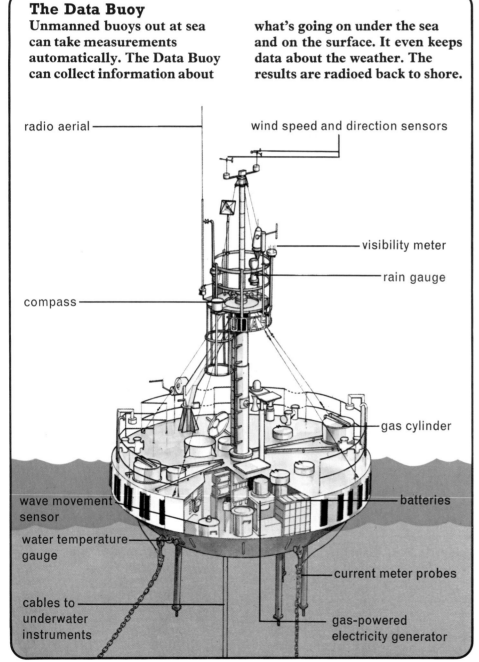

- radio aerial
- wind speed and direction sensors
- visibility meter
- rain gauge
- compass
- gas cylinder
- wave movement sensor
- batteries
- water temperature gauge
- current meter probes
- cables to underwater instruments
- gas-powered electricity generator

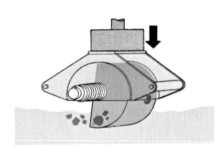

## The Shipek grab

This simple spring-loaded grab picks up lumps of rock or sediment from the seabed. It is lowered down gently on a rope. When it hits the bottom, the weight (arrowed) hits a trigger which releases the scoop.

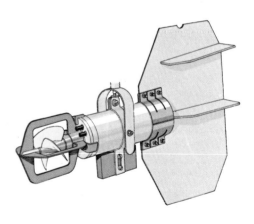

## The current meter

This instrument measures the speed and direction of underwater currents. It records the results on a miniature tape-recorder inside.

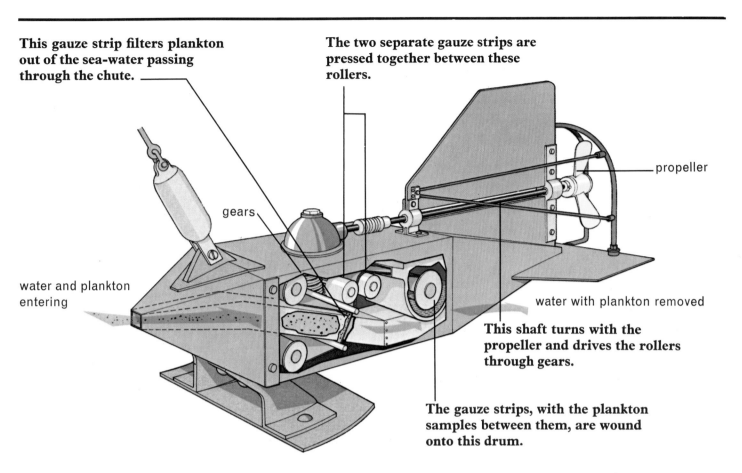

This gauze strip filters plankton out of the sea-water passing through the chute.

The two separate gauze strips are pressed together between these rollers.

propeller

gears

water and plankton entering

water with plankton removed

This shaft turns with the propeller and drives the rollers through gears.

The gauze strips, with the plankton samples between them, are wound onto this drum.

## The continuous plankton sampler

Many scientists believe that the study of plankton (microscopic forms of life) is the key to understanding more about fish and their movements. The plankton sampler is towed behind a research ship for long distances, collecting plankton. The samples are wound in through the front of the machine and pass along a chute. A strip of gauze goes across the chute and catches the plankton. Another strip of gauze traps the plankton against it. Sandwiched between the two gauze strips, the sample is wound onto a drum. When the sampler is brought to the surface the plankton is studied under a microscope.

---

This coil of copper tubing contains a special vapor. Its pressure falls as the temperature drops.

This small pressure gauge is connected to a needle which marks the smoked-glass screen.

The marks record the pressure of the vapor in the coil, and this tells you the water temperature.

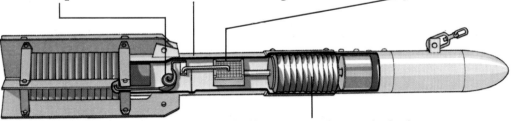

These bellows move the smoked-glass screen to record depth changes.

## The bathythermograph

The temperature of seawater changes as the depth increases. When a bathythermograph is lowered into the water, it plots a chart showing these temperature changes. You might wonder what use a chart like this is. To scientists taking precise measurements with echo sounders or sonars (see pages 34-5), a temperature chart is vital. Sound travels in water at different speeds, depending largely on the water temperature.

# The mineral storehouse

Salt is the most common mineral in the oceans, and the easiest to recover. Sea-water, left to evaporate in the heat of the sun in a shallow pool, will leave behind a thick crust of salt.

Sand and gravel are in such demand for building and road construction that some countries have found it worth the trouble to dredge them from the shallower parts of the ocean.

But the sea contains more precious substances than these. For example, rich deposits of metal-bearing ores are found on the shallower continental shelf regions. On the deep ocean floors there are huge quantities of manganese, nickel, copper and cobalt. These are found as fist-sized *nodules*. How they were formed, nobody really knows.

## New mining schemes

One day the industrial nations of the world will have to recover these vast seabed reserves. The obvious problems are the huge cost and the technical difficulties of raising them from the seabed. Large international mining companies are already working on schemes for deep ocean mining and for the new kinds of smelting plants that will be needed. But the problem of which nations will have the right to mine nodules is so serious that in 1973 the United Nations set up a conference to study the law of the sea. The aim is to make sure the whole world, not just the technologically advanced nations, will benefit from this resource.

### Remote-control dredging
**Manganese nodules are usually found about 5000 m (16,000 ft) deep. This means that any equipment used to mine them will have to be very strong to stand up to the water pressure. This dredger may one day bring nodules to the surface, completely processed! The operating crew will guide the dredger with the help of TV cameras.**

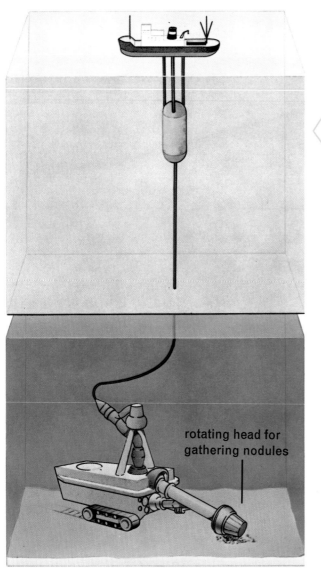

rotating head for gathering nodules

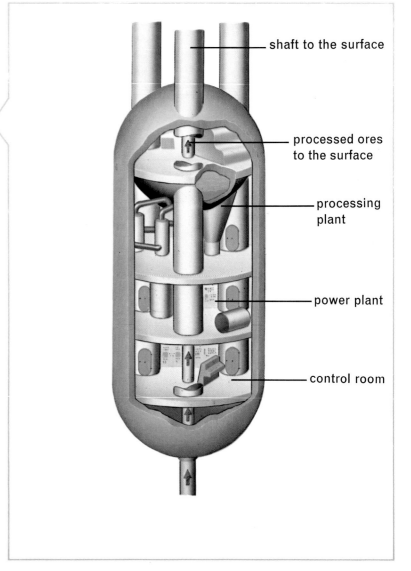

shaft to the surface

processed ores to the surface

processing plant

power plant

control room

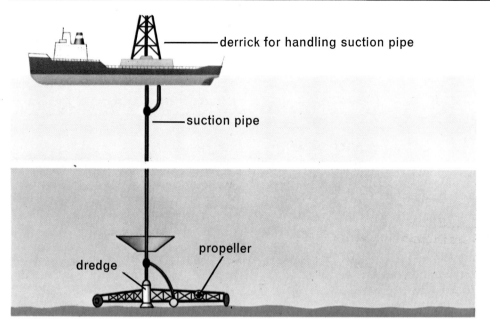

derrick for handling suction pipe

suction pipe

dredge

propeller

## Seabed vacuum cleaning
Deep-water vacuum cleaners are another possible way of collecting ores. They work in the same way as the airlift used by diving archaeologists (see pages 20-1). A huge length of flexible pipe connects the mining ship to a mobile underwater dredge. The dredge can be moved around in circles by the small propeller on the right. This sweeps the seabed, and what is collected is sucked back up the pipe.

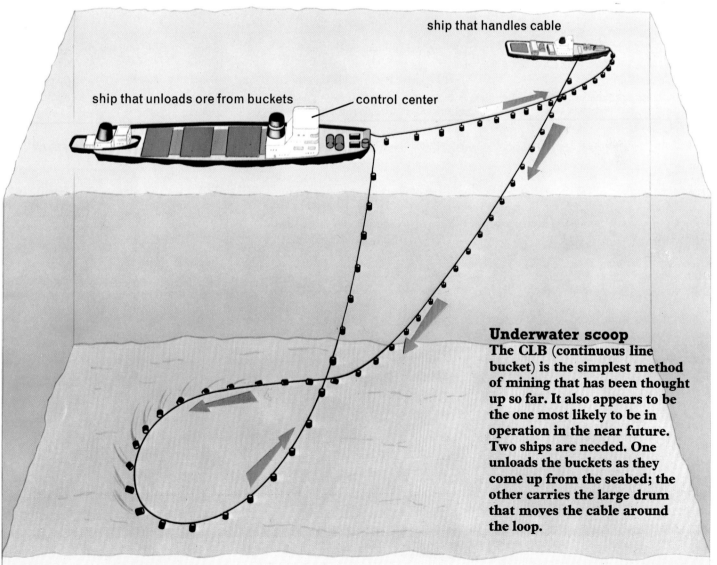

ship that handles cable

ship that unloads ore from buckets

control center

## Underwater scoop
The CLB (continuous line bucket) is the simplest method of mining that has been thought up so far. It also appears to be the one most likely to be in operation in the near future. Two ships are needed. One unloads the buckets as they come up from the seabed; the other carries the large drum that moves the cable around the loop.

# The hunt for oil and gas

The search for oil and gas is becoming more and more intense. It is one of the world's main sources of energy and so is very valuable to the countries in which it is found. The offshore oil prospector's first job is to find areas of the seabed rich in oil and gas, but without going to the expense of drilling. A technique called *seismic surveying*★ is used at this stage. But even a seismic survey cannot show beyond a shadow of doubt exactly where oil can be found under the sea.

## The exploration rig

The next stage is to drill exploration wells. But there are problems. In the North Sea, for instance, oil rigs are operating in up to 300 m (1000 ft) of water. The oil usually lies another 3000 m (10,000 ft) or more below the seabed. The surface of the sea is often very stormy so that adds to the difficulties too.

But even when an exploration well strikes oil, that isn't the end of the search. Several more drillings have to be made to decide whether there is enough oil to make it worth building a production platform. Even when a well is finished with, it has to be plugged with cement and all the seabed equipment removed to stop any interference with marine life or fishing.

*Staflo* is a 13,000-ton semi-submersible drilling rig. Tall legs support the drilling platform on huge pontoons (floating rafts) 20 m (65 ft) under the surface. The pontoons keep the rig steady even in rough weather, so drilling never has to stop.

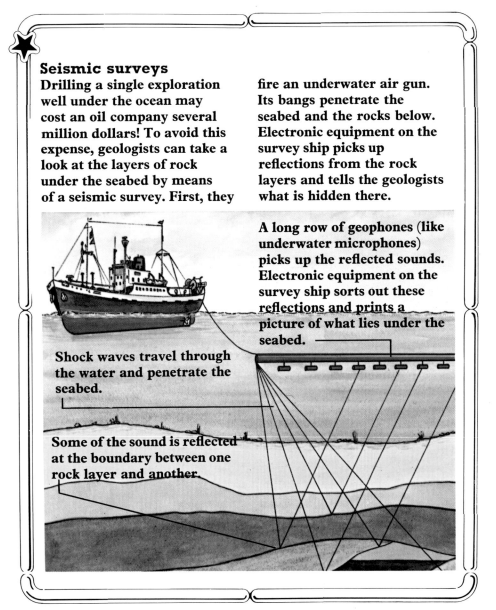

### Seismic surveys

Drilling a single exploration well under the ocean may cost an oil company several million dollars! To avoid this expense, geologists can take a look at the layers of rock under the seabed by means of a seismic survey. First, they fire an underwater air gun. Its bangs penetrate the seabed and the rocks below. Electronic equipment on the survey ship picks up reflections from the rock layers and tells the geologists what is hidden there.

A long row of geophones (like underwater microphones) picks up the reflected sounds. Electronic equipment on the survey ship sorts out these reflections and prints a picture of what lies under the seabed.

Shock waves travel through the water and penetrate the seabed.

Some of the sound is reflected at the boundary between one rock layer and another.

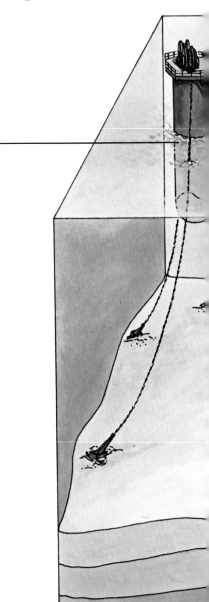

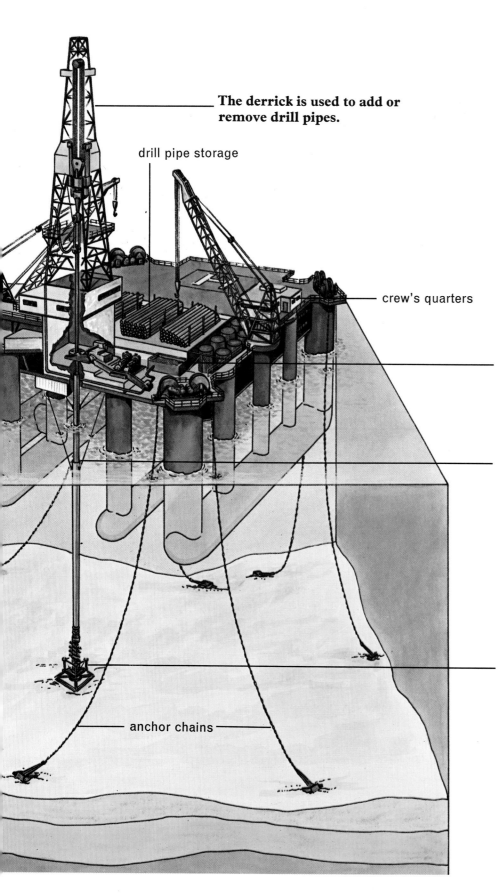

**The derrick is used to add or remove drill pipes.**

drill pipe storage

crew's quarters

anchor chains

As the drill goes deeper and deeper, new lengths of pipe have to be added. These men are using steel 'tongs' to handle the pipe.

Specially mixed 'mud' from this tank is pumped down to the tip of the drill. It cools the drill bit and picks up debris. Back on the surface, a geologist examines the debris to find out what kind of rock he is drilling.

The drill pipe is protected by this 'marine riser'. It has a telescopic joint that moves up and down with the rig.

The blow-out preventer closes automatically if the pressure in the well rises dangerously.

# Oil and gas production

Finding the oil and gas field is only the beginning of the story. The first stage of getting the oil to the refinery on the mainland is setting up a *production platform*. From here, production wells can be drilled, and the flow of oil to loading or storage points or to the mainland can be controlled. The platform also has to support its own crew—anything up to 100 men—and produce all its own power. It has to do this 24 hours a day, sometimes in terrible weather conditions. In the North Sea there are waves up to 25 m (80 ft) high and winds up to 200 km/h (125 mph).

## Gas from oil wells

Gas is an important by-product of oil operations. The southern part of the North Sea has wells that produce only gas. Some of the oil wells farther north also produce enough gas to take ashore for commercial use. The oil production platforms depend on gas from their own wells to drive the turbo-generators. These provide electricity to power the pumps that move the oil around. Any surplus gas that is not sent ashore or pumped back into the well is burned off in the atmosphere.

### Out to the drilling site

**Production platforms are sometimes called 'jackets'. A typical steel jacket in the North Sea can be more than 150 m (500 ft) from top to bottom and weigh more than 10,000 tons. Moving such a monster from the construction site to the offshore oil field is no easy job. Each stage of the operation has to be very carefully planned.**

**In the early stages of construction, a huge barge (marked in blue) is built on the floor of a large dry dock. The jacket is built, on its side, on top of the barge (1). When it's all ready, the dock gates can be opened. The barge and jacket float and can be towed out to sea (2). The tricky part comes when the barge and its load reach the oil field site. They have to be tipped upright and settled gently onto the seabed. The sections of the barge are flooded one by one, so that the engineers can control the angle, and the rate, at which the jacket sinks (3 and 4). This is all done by remote control from a nearby ship, because it isn't safe to be too near the platform as it sinks. When the jacket is finally in position the barge is taken away (5). It can be refloated and taken away to be used again.**

**The deck of the platform is prefabricated and is taken to the site later, on barges. It is lowered onto the jacket and secured. Last of all, the equipment for the platform and for crew accommodation are added (6).**

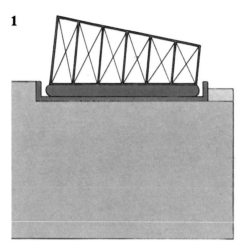

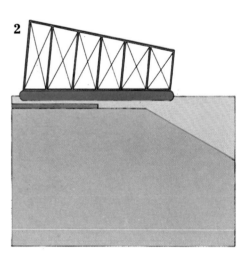

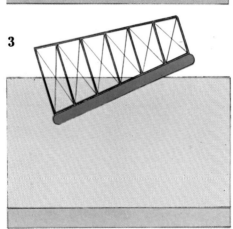

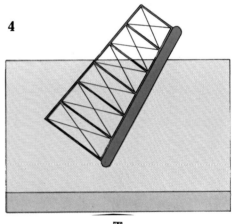

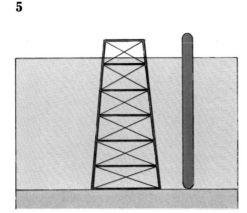

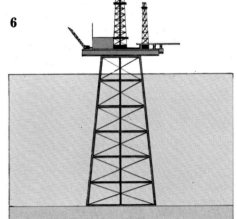

*Beryl A* is one of Mobil Oil's latest concrete production platforms to go into operation in the North Sea.

Concrete platforms are built in deep-water inlets and towed to the oil field in an upright position. To make them sink to the bottom, the cluster of storage tanks around the base of the legs is flooded.

Production wells can be drilled in all directions from a platform. Oil is usually found about 3000 m (10,000 ft) under the seabed. The drill is steered as it goes down to reach oil far away from the platform. The huge platform at the surface begins to look tiny in this scale-drawing compared to the depth the drill reaches.

The drilling pipes for the wells pass down through the legs of the platform. As many as 40 wells can be drilled from one platform!

# Transporting oil and gas ashore

Tankers can be used for a fair amount of oil transportation from the offshore oil field. But they are difficult to load in a rough sea. Some large oil fields use pipelines all the way from the platform to the shore. Smaller oil fields use pipelines to link up with neighboring platforms or offshore loading or storage points.

Undersea pipe-laying is a new technology all of its own which has grown to meet the needs of the offshore oil fields. Concrete-coated pipe in 12½ m (40 ft) lengths is ferried out from the shore to the most important vessel in the team, the pipe-laying barge. The separate lengths of pipe are welded into one single length on board the pipe-layer. Each weld is x-rayed to make sure it will stand up to the high pressure of oil or gas that the pipe will contain. The long length of pipe is then lowered out over the *stinger* at the stern of the barge.

## Seabed resting place

The pipeline isn't usually just left resting on the seabed. If it has to cross jagged rocks, the route has to be smoothed by dumping thousands of tons of ballast. In other places, the pipeline has to be laid in a trench dug by huge water-jet sleds.

**A diving barge stands by during the pipe-laying operation. The divers position the jet sled and make sure that the pipeline is laid correctly on the seabed.**

**The trench barge supplies high-pressure water to the jet sled, and draws it along the pipeline. When it's not being used, the sled hangs from the stern of the barge.**

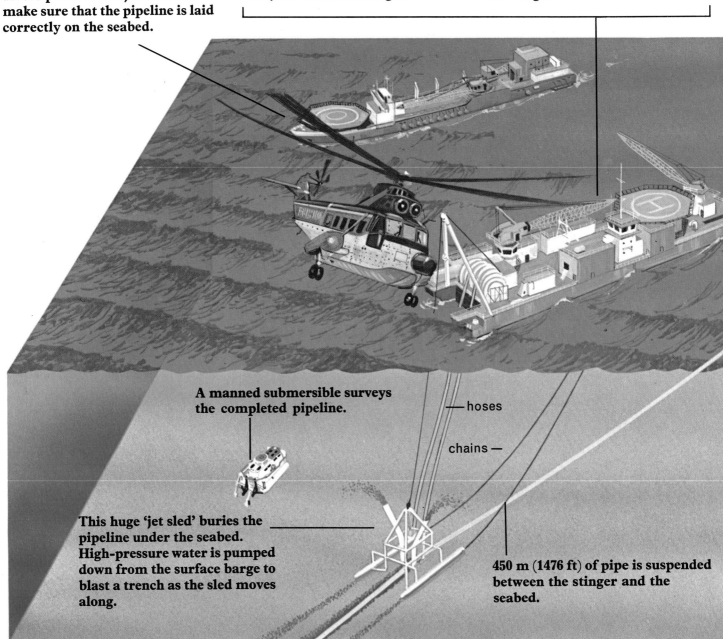

**A manned submersible surveys the completed pipeline.**

— hoses

chains —

**This huge 'jet sled' buries the pipeline under the seabed. High-pressure water is pumped down from the surface barge to blast a trench as the sled moves along.**

**450 m (1476 ft) of pipe is suspended between the stinger and the seabed.**

*Semac I* is a semi-submersible barge. It floats on huge pontoons which are far beneath the surface so that it can keep working even in rough weather.

The pipe-laying barge *Semac I* is specially built to work in the stormy North Sea.

Powerful tugs move the barge's anchors from time to time.

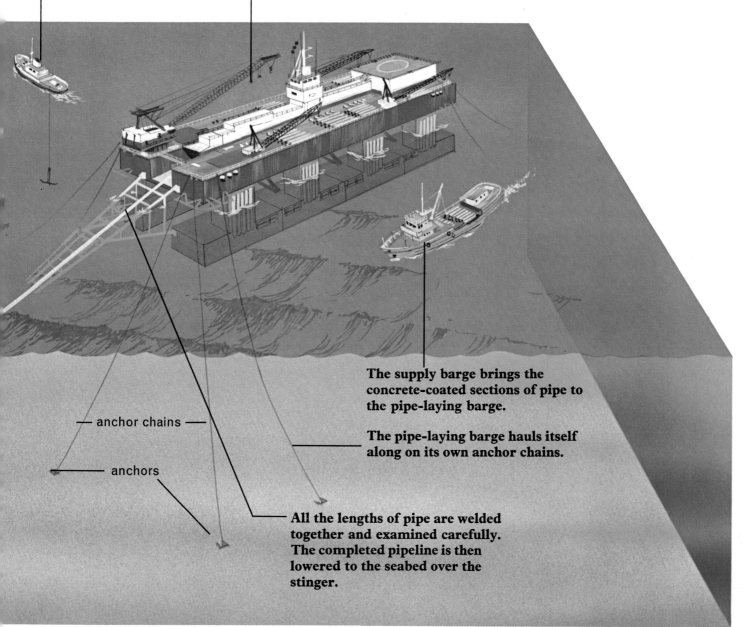

anchor chains

anchors

The supply barge brings the concrete-coated sections of pipe to the pipe-laying barge.

The pipe-laying barge hauls itself along on its own anchor chains.

All the lengths of pipe are welded together and examined carefully. The completed pipeline is then lowered to the seabed over the stinger.

# Food from the sea

More and more food has to be found to feed the world's growing population. At the moment 70 million tons of fish are brought ashore every year. Various techniques are used to catch these fish but scientists are always trying to make them more efficient.

## Finding the fish

Many fish are caught by trawlers. In the old days, the trawler skipper relied on his skill and experience to find the best fishing grounds. Now his skills are very different. He has to master a wide range of modern gadgets that help find the fish—from echo sounders to complicated net-handling gear.

*Fisheries research* is now carried out in many countries. The movement of plankton (the tiny creatures that fish feed on), and the way fish migrate to different parts of the sea are studied. This research provides the first clues to where the best fishing grounds are.

## Stern trawling

A huge bag-shaped net is pulled through the water. One kind of trawl catches the fish that live on the seabed. Another kind nets the fish shoals above the ocean floor. Otter boards control the shape and position of the trawl as it moves through the water.

French fishermen use a dip net off the coast of Brittany.

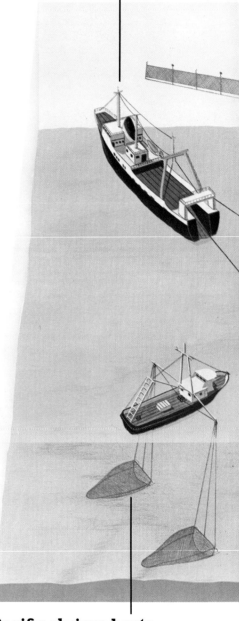

The trawler skipper checks these screens to find the fish shoals.

## Pacific shrimp boats

Two small trawl-like nets are drawn along the seabed. They hang from booms on either side of the fishing boat and catch shrimps and prawns.